DO YOU REALLY WANT

TO VISIT A RAINFOREST?

WRITTEN BY BRIDGET HEOS · ILLUSTRATED BY DANIELE FABBRI

RiverStream Science
Great Reading • Real Learning

Amicus Illustrated hardcover edition is published by
Amicus P.O. Box 1329, Mankato, MN 56002
www.amicuspublishing.us

RiverStream Publishing reprinted with permission of
Amicus Publishing.

Library of Congress Cataloging-in-Publication Data
Heos, Bridget, author.
 Do you really want to visit a rainforest? / by Bridget Heos ;
illustrated by Daniele Fabbri. — First edition.
     pages cm. — (Do you really want to visit...?)
 Audience: K-3.
 Summary: "A child goes on an adventure to the Amazon
Rainforest, discovering what the climate is like and
encountering some of the many species of animals and plants
that live in a tropical rainforest. Includes world map of
tropical rainforests and glossary"— Provided by publisher.
 Includes bibliographical references.
 ISBN 978-1-60753-453-2 (library binding) —
ISBN 978-1-60753-668-0 (ebook)
1. Rain forest ecology—Juvenile literature. 2. Rain forests—
Juvenile literature. I. Fabbri, Daniele, 1978- illustrator. II.
Title. III. Series: Do you really want to visit—?
QH541.5.R27H46 2015
577.34—dc23   2013028472

Editor: Rebecca Glaser
Designer: Kathleen Petelinsek

19 20 21 CG 21 20 19
RiverStream Publishing--Corporate Graphics,
Mankato, MN
ISBN 978-1-62243-223-3 (paperback)

ABOUT THE AUTHOR

Bridget Heos is the author of more than 60 books for children, including many Amicus Illustrated titles and her recent picture book *Mustache Baby* (Houghton Mifflin Harcourt, 2013). She lives on the prairie of Kansas City with her husband and four children.

ABOUT THE ILLUSTRATOR

Daniele Fabbri was born in Ravenna, Italy, in 1978. He graduated from Istituto Europeo di Design in Milan, Italy, and started his career as a cartoon animator, storyboarder, and background designer for animated series. He has worked as a freelance illustrator since 2003, collaborating with international publishers and advertising agencies.

So you want to visit a tropical rainforest. Are you sure? True, rainforests are full of amazing plants and animals. Some are beautiful, cute, or helpful. But others are a little scary. Plus tropical rainforests are hot, hot, hot.

Time to pack! You'll want to be prepared for the wet climate. You're off to the Amazon Rainforest in South America!

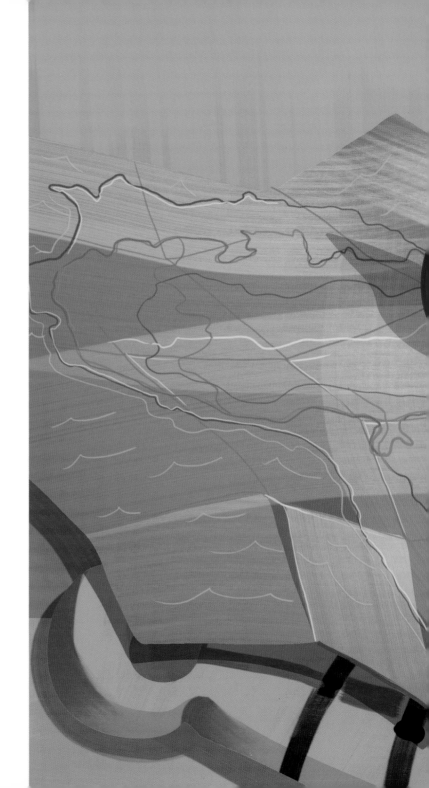

Once you're there, climb aboard a riverboat.
The jungle is thick with trees and plants and
there are not many roads.

The Amazon River and its tributaries are the best way to travel through the rainforest. The temperature hovers in the high 80s F (low 30s C), and it's very humid.

How about a swim with the pink river dolphins?
They are a dolphin species that lives in freshwater.

Aww look . . . that one is nuzzling you.

Wait a second. That one's not a dolphin. It's an electric eel! Quick, back inside the boat before it zaps you!

Watch the anacondas, piranhas, and stingrays. The Amazon has thousands of fish species—even more than the Atlantic Ocean.

It's getting dark. That's the perfect time to explore the jungle! It's when many animals wake up.

Look up! Way up! The trees—which grow 100 feet
(30 meters) tall—and the swinging vines are full of life.

A sloth wakes up in a kapok tree. It eats. Then it goes back to sleep. It sleeps so much that algae grows on its fur. It is camouflaged against the green leaves. A macaw dines on fruit from a palm tree. A jaguar crouches on a branch, ready to pounce.

Whew! The jaguar wasn't after you. It was
hunting a capybara, the world's largest rodent.
They weigh about 140 pounds (63.5 kg).

And now it's raining. Well, what did you expect? This is the rainforest. It rains 250 days a year for 100 inches (250 cm) total. Watch your step! Oh no, you scraped your arm.

Luckily the rainforest is home to many people. They live in villages by the river. And they grow helpful plants in their medicine gardens. This matico leaf will help stop the bleeding.

These Satare Maue people are starting a ritual. Would you like to watch?

The wooden gloves are filled with poison ants. The ants bite the older boys. It won't kill them. But it does hurt. It makes them tough. You have to be tough to survive in the rainforest. Right?

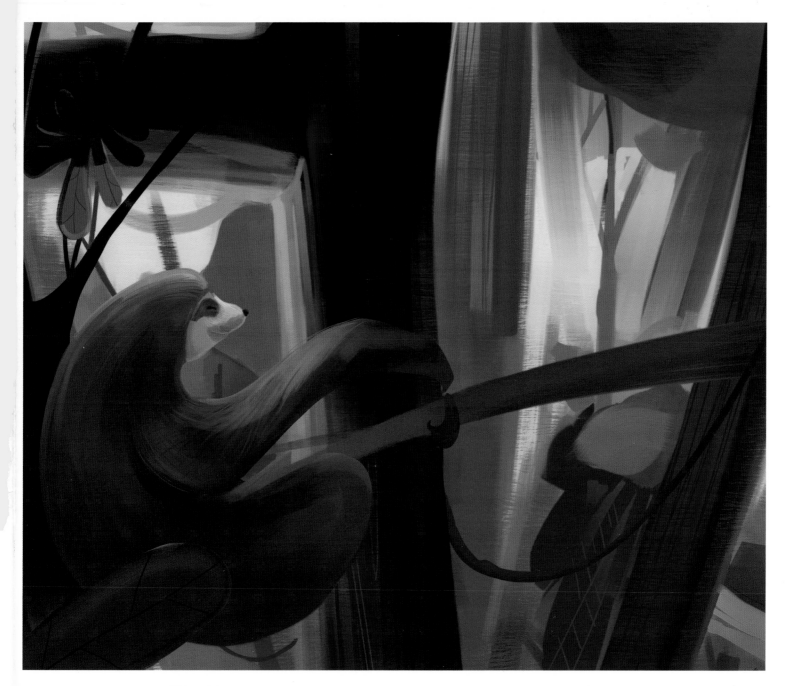

Well, either tough or very well camouflaged!

MAP OF WORLD TROPICAL RAINFORESTS

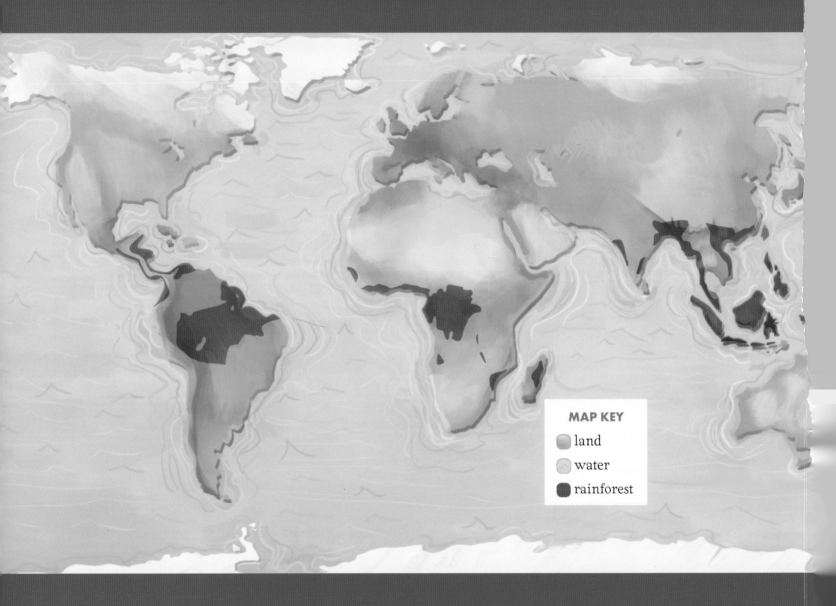

MAP KEY
- land
- water
- rainforest

PROTECT THE RAINFOREST

Trees in the rainforests are cut down for wood, or burned to allow cattle to graze or crops to grow. Some ways you can preserve the rainforest are:

- Buy locally grown and raised food.

- Conserve tree-based products, such as paper, by using two sides, and recycling it.

- Reuse furniture. Furniture is often made from tropical trees from rainforests. If you need a desk to do your homework, consider buying it at a garage sale, or accepting a hand-me-down.

GLOSSARY

camouflage Coloring that allows an animal to blend in with its surroundings.

freshwater Water in rivers and lakes, low in salt content, not in the oceans.

jungle A tropical forest.

palm A tree or shrub with fan-like fronds growing at the top.

rainforest An area with dense plant growth, including trees.

ritual A traditional ceremony to acknowledge a life change.

species A type of living thing, the members of which share important characteristics and can reproduce.

tributaries Rivers that feed or are fed by larger rivers.

READ MORE

Bodden, Valerie. *Amazon River.* Big Outdoors. Mankato, Minn.: Creative Education, 2010.

Hunter, Rebecca. **Rain Forests.** Eco Alert. Mankato, Minn.: Sea-to-Sea Publications, 2012.

Patkau, Karen. **Who Needs a Jungle?: A Rainforest Ecosystem.** Toronto: Tundra Books, 2012.

Simon, Seymour. **Tropical Rainforests.** New York: HarperCollins, 2010.

WEBSITES

Geography World by KBears.com
http://www.kbears.com/geography.html
Click on the globe to learn about world climates including rainforests, print maps of continents to color, and even listen to music from around the world.

Kids' Corner: Rainforest Alliance
http://www.rainforest-alliance.org/kids
Play games and learn more about rainforests around the world.

What's it Like Where You Live?: Rainforest Topics
http://www.mbgnet.net/sets/rforest/index.htm
View photos and read descriptions of rainforest plant and animal life, plus many more facts about rainforests.

Wildlife Webcams — Live from the Rainforest | World Land Trust
http://www.worldlandtrust.org/webcams
Watch rainforest birds live via webcams.

Every effort has been made to ensure that these websites are appropriate for children. However, because of the nature of the Internet, it is impossible to guarantee that these sites will remain active indefinitely or that their contents will not be altered.